MATT ZHANG

THE WOMAN OF ENNEAGRAM

1

LOVE AND SUCCESS EDITION

The woman of Enneagram 1: Love Marriage Success Edition

Enneagram For Women, Volume 1

Maria Rondon

Published by Maria Rondon, 2024.

ENNEAGRAM 1 FOR WOMEN.
Copyright © 2024 by Maria Rondon
All rights reserved. Printed in Catalunya, Spain.
No part of this book may be used or reproduced in any manner whatsoever without written permission except in the case of brief quotations embodied in critical articles and reviews. For information address Sans Serif Agency, Girona, Catalunya, Spain.
Sans Serif Agency Web Site: http://www.sansserifagency.com
Sans Serif Agency is a trademark of Sans Serif Agency.
Library of Congress Cataloging-in-Publication Data:
Rondon, Maria.
Enneagram 1 for women / Maria Rondon. — 1st ed.

While every precaution has been taken in the preparation of this book, the publisher assumes no responsibility for errors or omissions, or for damages resulting from the use of the information contained herein.

THE WOMAN OF ENNEAGRAM 1: LOVE MARRIAGE SUCCESS EDITION

First edition. March 27, 2024.

Copyright © 2024 Maria Rondon.

ISBN: 979-8224028337

Written by Maria Rondon.

SANS SERIF
EDITORIAL AGENCY

CONTENT

The History and Origins of the Enneagram: A brief historical overview of how the Enneagram developed and its relevance to self-knowledge.

- The Importance of Self-Knowledge for Women: Exploring how self-understanding benefits women in various aspects of their lives.

- ***Chapter 1: Love and Relationships***

-

- Navigating Type Differences in Relationships: How to understand and appreciate Enneagram type differences in relationships.
- Enneagram 1 and love Compatibility with other types
- The Dynamics of Subtypes in Romantic Relationships: Analyzing how subtypes (self-preservation, social, and sexual) influence romantic relationships.

- ***Chapter 2: Career and Purpose***

-

- Balance Between Personal and Professional Life: Strategies for maintaining a healthy balance between both spheres.
- Support Networks in the Workplace: The importance of building and maintaining supportive relationships at work.

- ***Chapter 3: Self-Esteem and Personal Growth***
- Facing the Fear of Failure: Techniques and exercises to overcome the fear of failure, a common obstacle for Type Ones.
- The Power of Resilience: Developing resilience in the face of challenges and internal criticism.

- ***Chapter 4: Health and Wellbeing***

-

- Integrating Conscious Nutrition: How conscious nutrition can support physical and emotional wellbeing.

- The Role of Physical Exercise in Stress Management: Discussing different forms of physical activity that can be beneficial for reducing stress.

- ### *Chapter 5: Motherhood and Parenting*
- Managing Perfectionism in Raising Children: How to balance expectations and foster a positive learning environment.
- Conscious and Present Parenting: Strategies for being present and consciously involved in parenting.

- ### *Chapter 6: Spirituality and Transcendence*
- The Enneagram and Connection to the Universe: Exploring how the Enneagram can be a tool for deepening spiritual connection.
- Diverse Spiritual Practices: Incorporating a variety of spiritual practices that may resonate with different readers.

- ### *CHAPTER 7: your wings*
- The Wings of Enneagram Type One: A section dedicated to exploring how the wings (Type 1w9 and Type 1w2) influence personality, preferences, and challenges.
- Integration and Disintegration Dynamics: How Type Ones integrate towards Type 7 (in growth) and disintegrate towards Type 4 (under stress), and strategies for managing these movements.

- ### *Conclusions and Additional Resources*

The History and Origins of the Enneagram

The Enneagram is an ancient system of personality typology that has been shrouded in mystery for centuries. Its precise origins are unknown, but it is believed to have roots tracing back to antiquity, with elements possibly originating from various spiritual and philosophical traditions around the world.

One of the earliest known mentions of the Enneagram symbol can be found in the writings of the ancient Pythagoreans and Neoplatonists in Greece, who used geometric figures and numbers to represent universal laws and truths. The nine-pointed enneagram figure, derived from the Greek words "ennea" meaning nine and "grammos" meaning something written or drawn, is thought to have held symbolic significance in their teachings.

However, the development of the Enneagram as a system for understanding human personalities was largely attributed to the work of the early 20th century thinkers George Gurdjieff and his student Peter Ouspensky. Gurdjieff, a Greek-Armenian spiritual teacher, is said to have learned about the Enneagram from sources within ancient esoteric traditions during his extensive travels in the East.

Through Ouspensky's writings in the 1930s, particularly the book "In Search of the Miraculous," the Enneagram symbol and its associations with personality types were introduced to a wider audience in the West. This sparked interest among psychologists, philosophers and spiritual seekers alike, who saw the Enneagram as a powerful tool for self-discovery and personal growth.

In the latter half of the 20th century, the Enneagram experienced a resurgence of popularity, thanks to the work of scholars and teachers like Claudio Naranjo, Oscar Ichazo and Helen Palmer. Each contributed their own insights, building upon the earlier foundations to expand the understanding of the nine personality types, their unique motivations, fears, and behavior patterns.

Today, the Enneagram is widely used not only for self-knowledge but also in fields such as counseling, business, education, and spiritual development. Its value lies in its ability to provide deep insights into the human psyche, fostering greater self-awareness, empathy and compassion for others.

At its core, the Enneagram serves as a guide for individuals to recognize their inherent strengths, blind spots, and defense mechanisms. By understanding one's Enneagram type and the unconscious patterns driving behavior, people can embark on a journey of transformation, shedding dysfunctional habits and aligning more fully with their highest potential.

The enduring relevance of the Enneagram stems from its capacity to reveal the universal aspects of human nature while honoring the uniqueness of each individual's experiences. As an integrative system, it offers a holistic framework for

The Importance of Self-Knowledge for Women: Exploring how self-understanding benefits women in various aspects of their lives

The importance of self-awareness for women through the Enneagram: Exploring how self-understanding benefits women in various aspects of their lives.

Self-awareness is a powerful tool in any individual's personal development arsenal, but for women, the Enneagram offers a unique path to self-understanding and empowerment. In a world where women often face contradictory expectations and multifaceted pressures, understanding themselves through the lens of the Enneagram can be revealing and transformative.

The Enneagram, with its roots in ancient spiritual and philosophical traditions, provides a detailed map of nine personality types, each with its own motivations, fears, and underlying desires. This system not only helps women identify their predominant behavior patterns but also offers insights into how these patterns influence their relationships, careers, and emotional well-being.

For many women, self-awareness through the Enneagram begins with identifying their main type. This process of self-discovery is not merely an act of labeling oneself but rather a step toward a deep understanding of their own complexities and internal contradictions. By understanding the roots of their automatic behaviors and emotional responses, women can begin to unravel the threads of limiting narratives they have woven throughout their lives.

In the realm of personal relationships, the Enneagram serves as a compass for navigating complex interpersonal dynamics. By understanding not only their own type but also the types of those around them, women can cultivate greater empathy and communication. This understanding can disarm conflicts, deepen connections, and foster an environment of mutual respect and understanding.

Professionally, the Enneagram offers women a lens through which they can assess their career aspirations and challenges. By identifying their inherent strengths and areas of potential growth, they can chart a path that is more aligned with their values and true goals. This self-awareness leads to authenticity in the workplace, allowing women to lead with confidence and pursue careers that reflect their true selves.

Emotionally, the journey through the Enneagram is often one of healing and self-acceptance. By confronting their fears and vulnerabilities, women can begin to break free from the chains of self-judgment and criticism. This process of self-inquiry and growth leads to greater resilience and deep inner peace, equipping women to handle life's ups and downs with grace and strength.

The Enneagram, therefore, is more than just a simple personality typing system. For women, it is a path to personal emancipation, a means to discover and embrace their unique authenticity. In this journey of self-awareness, women not only learn about themselves but also empower themselves to create lives that are genuinely fulfilling and purposeful.

The importance of self-awareness for women through the Enneagram cannot be underestimated. By exploring the depths of their being through this ancient system, women can unlock their unlimited potential, foster richer and more vibrant relationships, and confidently move forward into a future where their true selves shine with full force. Ultimately, the Enneagram offers not only a mirror in which to reflect but also a window into a life of greater fulfillment and authenticity.

CHAPTER 1
LOVE AND RELATIONSHIPS ENNEAGRAM TYPE 1

Navigating Type Differences in Relationships: Understanding and Appreciating Enneagram Type Differences in Relationships.

In the intricate dance of human relationships, personality differences not only add complexity but also enrich our interactions. Within this context, the Enneagram emerges as an invaluable compass, offering understanding and appreciation of these unique differences, particularly for Type 1 women, who, in their pursuit of perfection, may encounter challenges and opportunities in love and relationships.

Enneagram Type 1 women, known for their integrity, ethics, and self-control, often face the challenge of balancing their high personal standards with accepting the inherent imperfections in all human relationships. It is here that Enneagram knowledge becomes a tool for transformation, allowing not only self-acceptance but also openness to appreciate the unique qualities of others.

Exploring relationship dynamics through the lens of the Enneagram, it is essential to recognize that each type brings its own strengths, weaknesses, and behavioral tendencies. For example, while a Type 1 may value order and consistency, a Type 7 partner might seek variety and spontaneity. This contrast, though potentially a source of conflict, also offers fertile ground for mutual growth and personal enrichment if approached with understanding and respect.

The key to navigating these differences lies in authentic communication and empathy. By understanding the underlying motivations and fears of each Enneagram type, Type 1 women can learn to express their needs and expectations in a way that fosters connection rather than confrontation. Similarly, by being open to their partners' perspectives, they can discover new ways of seeing the world, thus softening their tendency toward critical judgment.

Furthermore, the self-awareness provided by the Enneagram empowers Type 1 women to work on their own areas of growth, such as the tendency to be overly critical of themselves and others. By recognizing that perfection is an unattainable ideal, they can begin to value the process and beauty of imperfections, both in themselves and in their relationships.

The Enneagram also illuminates the path to understanding and patience, especially important for Type 1 women who may struggle with impatience toward others' differences. Learning to value these differences as complementary rather than threatening can transform relationships in profound and lasting ways.

Ultimately, Type 1 women will find that true love and connection stem from genuine acceptance, both of oneself and of the other. By embracing Enneagram type differences in their relationships, they not only enrich their understanding of the human spectrum but also open themselves to richer and more meaningful experiences.

Understanding and appreciating Enneagram type differences in relationships is, therefore, a journey to the very heart of what it means to love and be loved. For Type 1 women, this journey promises not only the fulfillment of deeper and more authentic relationships but also an invitation to embrace imperfection as an essential and beautiful part of the human experience. In this space of shared vulnerability and mutual understanding, true love flourishes, revealing the transformative power of self-awareness and acceptance.

The Dynamics of Enneagram Type 1 in Romantic Relationships: Analyzing how the subtypes (self-preservation, social, and sexual) influence romantic relationships.

In the complex tapestry of romantic relationships, Enneagram Type 1 women navigate waters marked by the pursuit of perfection, not only within themselves but also in their partners and the dynamics of their relationship. This journey towards love and connection is deeply influenced by the self-preservation, social, and sexual subtypes, each bringing distinctive nuances that affect how these relationships unfold and are experienced.

Self-Preservation Subtype

Type 1 women with a self-preservation subtype tend to focus on security and stability within their romantic relationships. Their quest for perfection manifests in creating a harmonious home and a structured lifestyle. However, this desire may lead them to exert control over the environment and daily routines, which can create tensions if their partner craves more spontaneity. To harmonize these contrasts, open communication is essential, where they express their needs and find a balance between structure and flexibility. Understanding that perfection is not the only path to happiness is a crucial step in their personal development and strengthening their relationship.

Social Subtype

The social subtype in Type 1 women is characterized by their focus on community and the welfare of others, including a deep dedication to meaningful relationships. Their ideal of perfection extends to the image they project as a couple and how this contributes to the world around them. Although this orientation towards mutual service can strengthen bonds, it can also lead to neglecting individual needs in pursuit of an idealized image. The challenge for these women is to recognize and honor their own desires and those of their partner as integral parts of an authentic and deeply connected relationship.

Sexual Subtype

Type 1 women with a sexual subtype channel intense energy into their intimate relationships, seeking a connection and passion that meets their elevated ideal of perfection. This passion can be a double-edged sword; on one hand, it fuels the depth and intimacy of the relationship, but on the other hand, it can lead to unrealistic expectations about emotional and physical connection. The key for women of this subtype is to learn to value imperfection as part of the shared journey, finding beauty in moments of vulnerability and authentic connection beyond unattainable ideals.

In all these dynamics, the Enneagram serves as a beacon, illuminating the path towards a deeper understanding of themselves and how they interact in the realm of love. By delving into the subtypes and how they influence their romantic relationships, Type 1 women can begin to peel back the layers of self-imposed expectations and norms, opening up to the richness of experiences and emotions that imperfect human relationships have to offer.

This journey towards true love and fulfilling relationships, guided by Enneagram knowledge, is an invitation for Type 1 women to embrace imperfection not as a flaw, but as a gateway to genuine connection and mutual acceptance. In this process of transformation, they learn that true perfection is not found in the absence of flaws, but in the ability to love and be loved in all their complex humanity.

Enneagram Type 1 and Romantic Compatibility

In the journey towards deep self-understanding and understanding the dynamics of our relationships, the Enneagram stands out as an invaluable compass, especially for Type 1 women, who seek harmony and perfection not only in their surroundings but also in their romantic relationships. This chapter delves into the world of love and compatibility from the perspective of Enneagram Type 1, unraveling how their intrinsic traits intertwine with those of other types in the pursuit of meaningful and profound connections.

Enneagram Type 1, known for its integrity, rigorous ethics, and commitment to constant improvement, approaches love with the same seriousness and determination that characterizes its approach to other

aspects of life. However, this quest for perfection can be both its greatest strength and its most significant challenge in romantic relationships.

Romantic compatibility for Type 1 is not merely about finding someone who meets a meticulously curated list of criteria, but rather about cultivating a relationship where both parties can grow, learn, and above all, accept each other in their inherent imperfection. This profound understanding of compatibility becomes the foundation upon which Type 1 women can build lasting and enriching relationships.

Compatibility with Other Enneagram Types

The interaction of Type 1 with other Enneagram types reveals a rich tapestry of potential romantic dynamics, each with its own lessons and opportunities for personal growth. Below, we explore how these dynamics may manifest in some of the most common pairings:

Type 1 and Type 2: This pair is often bound by a deep sense of duty and a desire to help others. While Type 1 focuses on correction and improvement, Type 2 seeks to meet their partner's needs, creating a balance of support and mutual encouragement. However, it is crucial for both to learn to communicate their own needs to avoid resentments and misunderstandings.

Type 1 and Type 9: The serenity and acceptance of Type 9 can be a calming counterbalance to the intensity and self-criticism of Type 1. Together, they can find a haven of peace and stability. However, it is important for Type 1 to avoid imposing too many expectations of perfection on Type 9, who values harmony and may yield too much.

Type 1 and Type 1: A couple composed of two Type 1 individuals can be a bastion of commitment and shared values. However, their common tendency towards perfectionism and self-criticism can lead to a dynamic where pressure to meet impossible standards undermines the joy and spontaneity of the relationship. Learning to celebrate small imperfections as part of their shared journey is key.

Romantic compatibility for Type 1, therefore, focuses less on finding the 'perfect' partner and more on developing a relationship where both they and their partners can accept and grow together in a space of unconditional love and mutual understanding. By recognizing and valuing the unique differences of each Enneagram type, Type 1 women can navigate the landscape of love with a deeper appreciation for the diversity and richness that these differences bring to their relationships.

In this journey towards true love and compatibility, the Enneagram not only offers Type 1 women a guide to understanding themselves and their partners more clearly but also provides them with the tools to cultivate relationships where perfection is not the ultimate goal, but acceptance, shared growth, and mutual joy. Ultimately, the path to romantic compatibility is enriched by the recognition that our imperfections are what make us human, and it is in our shared humanity where we find true love.

CHAPTER 2

Career and Purpose

Balancing Personal and Professional Life: Strategies for maintaining a healthy balance between both spheres.

For Enneagram Type 1 women, the pursuit of excellence and perfection extends to both their professional and personal lives. Known for their unwavering work ethic, commitment to continuous improvement, and meticulous attention to detail, these women face the unique challenge of maintaining a healthy balance between their dedication to work and the care of their emotional well-being and personal relationships.

The Type 1's tendency to set high standards and propensity for self-criticism can, without proper care, lead to an imbalance that negatively impacts both their personal happiness and professional effectiveness. However, by applying the same rigor and commitment with which they pursue excellence in their work to the task of cultivating a work-life balance, Type 1 women can find harmony that enriches all aspects of their lives.

Recognition of Personal Limits

The first step towards achieving this balance is recognizing one's own limits. For Type 1, admitting that absolute perfection is an unattainable ideal, both at work and at home, can be liberating. This acknowledgment allows for a more flexible and compassionate approach to goals and responsibilities, thereby facilitating a more equitable distribution of energy and time.

Establishment of Clear Priorities

Determining what truly matters is crucial for Type 1 women. This involves regularly evaluating their values, goals, and what they find most rewarding and meaningful in life. By setting clear priorities, they can make more informed decisions about how and where to focus their efforts, ensuring that both their professional aspirations and personal needs receive the attention they deserve.

Implementation of Flexible Routines

Routines can provide a comforting structure for Type 1, helping them organize their time efficiently. However, the key is flexibility; routines should serve as guides, not chains. Integrating moments of rest, leisure, and connection with loved ones into their schedule is not only essential for their well-being but also enhances their long-term productivity and creativity.

Practice of Self-Compassion and Self-Care

Self-care is a fundamental aspect of maintaining a healthy balance. Type 1 women must practice self-compassion, reminding themselves that it is okay to take a break, enjoy leisure moments, and forgive themselves for not meeting unrealistic expectations. Nurturing the body, mind, and spirit with activities that promote relaxation and joy is as important as fulfilling any work task.

Open Communication in Relationships

Finally, open and honest communication with colleagues, friends, and family is essential. Expressing their needs, setting healthy boundaries, and seeking support when necessary not only fosters stronger and more meaningful relationships but also contributes to a more harmonious work environment and home.

For Type 1 women of the Enneagram, balancing personal and professional life is not a final destination, but a continuous journey of self-awareness and growth. By applying their innate leadership ability and commitment to improvement not only to their careers but also to their own well-being, they can create a fulfilling and satisfying life where excellence and happiness are not mutually exclusive but complementary aspects of an authentic and balanced existence. In this process, the Enneagram serves as an invaluable tool, providing the perspective and understanding necessary to navigate this balance with grace and wisdom.

"Support Networks in the Workplace: The reasons which lie behind the need for creating and keeping strong connections in a work place.

While the Road of The Enneagram is about self-discovering of self and growth that changes women of Type 1 in terms of their inner motif, fears, and virtues in regard to career goals and the general life purpose. In strive for righteousness between humans this female type holds where chaos is going to be removed, efficiency is improved and standards are met is the rightful place. While the effect of their job competency on their professional prosperity is often outshined, there is another important factor that is usually ignored: development of the support networks in the workplace.

Supportive relationships are the vital pillars of Job satisfaction; hence, Type1s cannot afford to underplay their importance in work environment. The roles of coaches, peers and mentors come out as crucial components of the environment where perfectionism and self-criticism can sometime shadow their achievements. Individuals can count on the small network of co-workers and mentors to provide praises, instructions, and friendships, which becomes very crucial. They are as the stepping stones for professional improvement as well as an inclusive shield against the probable detachment that comes from their very high set bar.

Network building is about creating those bonds with people who share the same values and goals and those who possess certain traits that Type 1 women can utilize and carry forth. The first element of this process implies that people no longer regard themselves as islands no matter they take Enneagram type. People co-operation, reciprocal respect and empathy are the highest values in caring for any favourable workforce system. Through living these principles, Type 1 women can build communicative ties with colleagues, superiors, and indeed, their juniors, bonding a sense of mutual interest and commitment.

Besides, it might happen that this is just not enough to go on but these relationships need to be pushed and nurtured. Type I women have also been encouraged to practice vulnerability by telling those who are close to them about themselves which includes who they are, what they perceive as their challenges and their ambitions. This process in turn is bound to reward the women with reciprocal support. Establishing a structured and effective system of communication, whether through formal gatherings or regular talks, allows and supports the network to remain reliable and prompt at all times to the needs of its members.

Indeed, any support network, once well-established, has a positive impact on any consumer in innumerable ways. Professional wise, it enables networking through mentoring, collaboration, and chances of improving one's career experience. Caring for others not only has a positive impact on others but also boosts the caregiver's mental health. It minimizes stress, making caregivers happier and more satisfied with their work. Additionally, a network of relationships of Type 1 women give them various ideas, making them question and consider other views, and this, in turn, gives them more understanding, ample options and better decisions.

While investing in developing strong social networks of Type 1 women is essential for successfully manifesting their career and life purpose, these networks play a crucial role in empowering women to navigate the complexities of the workplace. Besides this, these networks give them a feeling of their self-worth and they are able to transform their ideas into realties from which they move on with confidence and honesty. Through investing in the development of supporting workplace relationships, Type 1 women can make their careers a better experience, one in which success is not only a result of individual efforts, but also is achieved as part of the collective synergy of a cohesive team.

The way to create and care for a sustaining-in-the-workplace support networks is the powerfully example what the understanding of your Enneagram type is capable of. If it is Type 1 ladies who I am talking about, interpersonal relationship is a major consideration in professional place and therefore it is very crucial that they take this as a threshold to have a career that is consistent with their values and dreams. And as they keep going along their way these links stand as a manifestation of their ability to change, adapt and accomplish a cooperative society that is much beneficial, productive and effective.

CHAPTER 3

Self-Esteem and Personal Growth

"Facing the Fear of Failure: Techniques and Exercises to Clear the Goal of Failure, the Most Common Difficulties that Type Ones may Face"

Enneagram female Type One's often overcome the terrible fear of failing, which is the huge mountain that can prevent the development and altogether of confidence. This fear shows an inner longing to achieve the highest degree of excellence, order and righteousness. Whilst these characteristics are the what that inspires Type A individuals to strive for excellence, they could also cause them self-criticism and a crippling fear of mistakes. Being able to acknowledge and indeed overcome these fears is key for the Type Ones to open new doors in their self-development and travel on the path to personal positive development.

How to Overcome the Fear of Failing

Reframing Failure: With that in mind, shift your point of view towards failure. Don't look at failure as something to condemn or be condemned by. It is this opportunity for learning that is priceless. Rather than killing the growth mindset by constantly demeaning yourself based on the question "how can I always avoid making mistakes?", try to reframe it with the question, "what can I learn from this experience?"

Setting Realistic Expectations: Type Ones are a group of people who often set themselves such astronomically high standards that this may elicit unrealistic expectations easily beyond what a human can achieve. Setting appropriate expectations is of great importance. It is just as important to adjust these expectations to more realistic levels. For example, plan easier goals to reach, which you can feel proud of your progress, instead of only focusing on the ultimate result. Praise yourself when you succeed doing something and this will motivate you and make you brave in trying.

Mindfulness and Acceptance: Techniques involving mindfulness, for instance, meditating and taking deep breaths help realize the level of the anxiety that can arise by the fear of failure to some extent. They cultivate this state of feeling instantly and keeping you in tune with the present.

thoughts and feelings without judgment. Over time, mindfulness helps cultivate a sense of inner peace and reduces the tendency towards self-criticism.

Self-Compassion Exercises: Self-compassion is a powerful antidote to the fear of failure. One exercise to cultivate self-compassion involves writing a letter to yourself from the perspective of a kind, understanding friend. In this letter, acknowledge your feelings of fear and disappointment without criticism, offer support, and remind yourself of your worth and capabilities. This practice encourages a more forgiving and compassionate self-dialogue.

Exposure to Failure: While it may seem counterintuitive, gradually exposing yourself to situations where failure is a possibility can desensitize you to the fear. Start with low-risk situations and work your way up. Reflect on each experience, focusing on what you learned and how you can apply those lessons in the future. This exposure builds resilience and reduces the power that fear of failure holds over you.

Seek Support: Building a support network of friends, family, or professionals who understand and encourage your journey is invaluable. Sharing your experiences and fears with others can provide new perspectives, reduce feelings of isolation, and offer encouragement when you're struggling with self-doubt.

By implementing these techniques and exercises, Type One women can begin to dismantle the fear of failure that inhibits their self-esteem and personal growth. Embracing failure as a natural part of the learning process allows for a more forgiving self-assessment and paves the way for a journey filled with growth, self-discovery, and the realization of their true, authentic selves. In this journey, the Enneagram serves not only as a guide but also as a companion, offering insights and strategies to navigate the complexities of personal development with grace and resilience.

The Power of Resilience: Developing Resilience in the Face of Challenges and Internal Criticism"

For women who identify with the Enneagram Type 1, the path to self-esteem and personal growth is often paved with the pursuit of perfection and a critical inner voice. This pursuit, while it drives them towards high standards and integrity, can also lead to feelings of inadequacy when those standards are not met. The key to navigating this path with grace and strength lies in the development of resilience—a quality that enables individuals to face challenges, learn from failures, and persevere in the face of internal and external criticism.

Resilience is not an innate trait but a skill that can be developed and strengthened over time. For Type 1 women, building resilience involves several key strategies that allow them to harness their critical nature in a way that fosters growth, self-compassion, and adaptability.

Understanding and Reframing the Inner Critic

The first step in building resilience is to understand and reframe the role of the inner critic. For Type 1s, the inner critic can be a harsh voice that amplifies fears of failure and imperfection. By recognizing that this voice stems from a desire for excellence and not a fundamental flaw in their character, Type 1 women can begin to reframe their inner dialogue. Instead of succumbing to the critic, they can engage with it constructively, asking, "What can I learn from this?" rather than "What did I do wrong?"

Embracing Imperfection

Embracing imperfection is a powerful exercise in developing resilience. Type 1 women can practice this by setting intentional "imperfection goals," small tasks or activities where the outcome is deliberately less than perfect. This practice helps to desensitize the fear of making mistakes and fosters a more forgiving approach to self-evaluation and growth.

Cultivating a Growth Mindset

A growth mindset, the belief that abilities and intelligence can be developed through dedication and hard work, is crucial for building resilience. Type 1 women can cultivate this mindset by celebrating efforts and progress, not just outcomes. Recognizing the value in the process of learning and growing helps to mitigate the fear of failure and encourages a more adaptable and resilient approach to challenges.

Seeking Support and Connection

Building resilience does not mean going it alone. On the contrary, seeking support and connection is a vital part of this journey. For Type 1 women, forming relationships with individuals who offer encouragement, understanding, and a different perspective can provide a much-needed counterbalance to their inner critic. Whether it's through professional support, like therapy or coaching, or personal support systems, such as friends or family, these connections reinforce the message that they are valued for who they are, not just for what they achieve.

Practicing Self-Care and Compassion

Finally, resilience is nurtured through self-care and compassion. For Type 1 women, this means allowing themselves the same kindness and understanding they would offer to others. Incorporating self-care routines, setting boundaries, and practicing self-compassion exercises are all ways to reinforce their worthiness and resilience.

Developing resilience in the face of challenges and internal criticism is a dynamic and ongoing process. For Enneagram Type 1 women, this journey involves embracing imperfection, cultivating a growth mindset, and nurturing supportive relationships. By doing so, they can transform their critical nature into a source of strength, enabling them to face life's challenges with courage and confidence. In this process of transformation, the true power of resilience is realized—not as a shield against vulnerability, but as a wellspring of growth, adaptability, and self-acceptance.

Through the lens of the Enneagram, Type 1 women are equipped with a unique set of tools for personal development. As they learn to harness the power of resilience, they pave the way for a journey marked by self-discovery, fulfillment, and the realization of their true, authentic selves.

CHAPTER 4
Health and Wellbeing

Integrating Conscious Nutrition: How Conscious Nutrition Can Support Physical and Emotional Wellbeing

In the pursuit of health and wellbeing, conscious nutrition emerges as a pivotal element, especially for individuals navigating the complexities of their Enneagram Type 1 personalities. Type 1s, often driven by ideals of perfection and self-discipline, can benefit profoundly from integrating conscious nutrition into their lives. This practice not only supports physical health but also plays a crucial role in emotional and psychological wellbeing.

Conscious nutrition is the mindful selection and consumption of food that nourishes the body, mind, and spirit. It transcends mere dietary choices, encompassing a holistic approach that recognizes the interconnectedness of our food, our health, and the world around us. For Type 1s, who strive for integrity and balance, conscious nutrition offers a path to harmonize their inner standards with their outer actions.

The Physical Benefits of Conscious Nutrition

At the core of conscious nutrition is the understanding that the food we eat directly impacts our physical health. For Type 1s, the emphasis on quality, purity, and wholesomeness aligns with their intrinsic values. Incorporating a variety of nutrient-dense foods, such as fruits, vegetables, whole grains, lean proteins, and healthy fats, supports optimal body function. This nutritional approach can enhance energy levels, improve digestive health, and reduce the risk of chronic diseases, offering Type 1s the vitality needed to pursue their goals with vigor and determination.

The Emotional and Psychological Impact

Beyond physical health, conscious nutrition profoundly affects emotional and psychological wellbeing. Type 1s, who often experience an internal struggle between their high standards and the reality of imperfection, can find solace in the practice of mindful eating. By focusing on the sensory experience of eating, appreciating the flavors, textures, and aromas of their food, Type 1s can cultivate a more compassionate and forgiving relationship with themselves.

Moreover, the act of choosing foods that are not only healthy for the individual but also sustainable for the planet resonates with Type 1s' desire to make ethically responsible choices. This alignment between personal values and actions can foster a sense of purpose and fulfillment, mitigating feelings of guilt or inadequacy that may arise from perceived failures.

Strategies for Integrating Conscious Nutrition

Mindful Eating: Begin by cultivating mindfulness during meals. Pay attention to the act of eating, noticing the taste, texture, and aroma of your food. This practice helps foster a deeper connection to your food and its impact on your body, encouraging a more thoughtful approach to eating.

Educate Yourself: Knowledge is power. Learning about the nutritional value of different foods and understanding how they affect your body can empower Type 1s to make informed decisions that align with their health goals and ethical standards.

Plan and Prepare: For Type 1s, the structure can be incredibly supportive. Planning meals and preparing food in advance ensure that you have healthy, nourishing options on hand, reducing the temptation to make less conscious choices.

Reflect on Your Food Choices: Regular reflection on your eating habits can provide insights into how your food choices affect your physical and emotional wellbeing. This reflection can also help identify areas for improvement, allowing you to adjust your approach to conscious nutrition as needed.

Seek Balance: Remember, perfection is not the goal. Striving for balance and moderation in your diet acknowledges the complexity of human needs and desires. Allowing yourself the flexibility to enjoy a wide range of foods without guilt or judgment can lead to a healthier, more sustainable relationship with nutrition.

For Enneagram Type 1 women, integrating conscious nutrition into their lives offers a powerful avenue for enhancing their physical health, emotional wellbeing, and overall sense of fulfillment. By aligning their dietary choices with their core values, they can navigate the journey towards health and wellbeing with grace, compassion, and purpose, embodying the true essence of their personality type.

The Role of Physical Exercise in Stress Management

Physical exercise is a powerful antidote to stress, benefiting both the mind and body. It stimulates the production of endorphins, the brain's feel-good neurotransmitters, which act as natural painkillers and mood elevators. Moreover, regular physical activity can improve overall cognitive function and reduce the symptoms of anxiety and depression, making it an essential component of a holistic approach to wellbeing for Type 1 women.

Different Forms of Physical Activity Beneficial for Reducing Stress

Mindful Movement Practices: Yoga and Tai Chi are exemplary mindful movement practices that blend physical activity with meditation, enhancing not only physical strength and flexibility but also promoting mental clarity and emotional calm. These practices encourage Type 1 women to focus on the present moment, fostering a sense of serenity and reducing the tendency to dwell on past mistakes or worry about future imperfections.

Aerobic Exercises: Activities such as running, cycling, swimming, or brisk walking can be particularly effective for stress management. They help improve cardiovascular health, boost energy levels, and provide an outlet for releasing pent-up tension. For Type 1 women, the rhythmic nature of these activities can also serve as a meditative practice, helping to clear the mind and bring about a sense of inner balance.

Strength Training: Engaging in strength training or resistance exercises can empower Type 1 women by improving physical resilience, which in turn, reinforces mental and emotional strength. The focus required during these activities can divert attention away from stressors, offering a constructive outlet for the drive towards perfectionism by channeling it into personal physical achievements.

Outdoor Activities: Immersing oneself in nature through hiking, gardening, or simply taking walks in natural settings can significantly reduce stress levels. The natural environment offers a unique sense of tranquility and perspective that can help Type 1 women reconnect with the simplicity and beauty of the present moment, distancing themselves from the critical inner voice that drives their stress.

Group Sports and Classes: Participating in group sports, dance classes, or fitness groups can provide social support, enhancing the stress-reducing benefits of exercise. The camaraderie and shared experiences can help Type 1 women feel less isolated in their struggles, offering a sense of belonging and mutual encouragement.

Incorporating a variety of physical activities into their routine allows Type 1 women to find the forms of exercise that resonate most deeply with their individual needs and preferences. The key is to approach physical exercise not as another domain for perfectionism but as a source of joy, relaxation, and self-care.

For Type 1 women on the Enneagram journey, embracing physical exercise as a tool for stress management can be transformative. It offers a practical way to balance their drive for perfection with the need for self-compassion and emotional wellbeing. By integrating conscious nutrition and physical activity into their lives, Type 1 women can cultivate resilience, enhance their health, and progress towards realizing their true, authentic selves, where health and wellbeing form the bedrock of personal growth and fulfillment.

CHAPTER 5

Motherhood and Parenting

Managing Perfectionism in Raising Children: How to Balance Expectations and Foster a Positive Learning Environment"

For Type 1 women on the Enneagram, known for their high standards, strong sense of right and wrong, and a deep commitment to integrity, motherhood introduces a unique set of challenges and rewards. The innate desire for perfectionism that Type 1s carry into various aspects of their lives can also seep into their parenting style. While striving to provide the best for their children is commendable, the pursuit of perfection in parenting can create undue stress for both mother and child. Recognizing and managing this perfectionism is crucial in raising children in a way that balances expectations and fosters a positive, nurturing learning environment.

Understanding the Impact of Perfectionism in Parenting

Perfectionism can manifest in parenting as an unyielding expectation for flawless behavior, exceptional achievement, and constant compliance from children. For Type 1 mothers, this can lead to a rigid parenting style that leaves little room for the natural exploration, mistakes, and learning processes essential to a child's development. It's important to recognize that children thrive in environments where they feel loved and accepted for who they are, not just for their accomplishments or adherence to rules.

Strategies for Balancing Expectations

Embrace Imperfection: One of the most liberating steps a Type 1 mother can take is to embrace imperfection, both in herself and her children. Acknowledge that making mistakes is a natural part of growth and learning. Share stories of your own failures and how you learned from them, showing your children that imperfection is not only acceptable but valuable.

Focus on Effort Rather Than Outcome: Shift the focus from achieving perfect results to valuing effort and improvement. Celebrate the hard work your children put into their tasks, regardless of the outcome. This approach helps build resilience and a healthy work ethic, teaching children that persistence and effort are more important than flawless performance.

Create a Safe Space for Emotional Expression: Encourage your children to express their emotions, fears, and frustrations without fear of judgment or punishment. A home environment where feelings are openly discussed and validated fosters emotional intelligence and resilience in children.

Practice Flexible Parenting: While structure and rules are important, being flexible can lead to happier and more adaptable children. Be willing to adjust your expectations and rules as your children grow and their needs change. This flexibility demonstrates to your children that you respect their individuality and are responsive to their development.

Model Self-Compassion: Children learn by example. By practicing self-compassion and forgiving yourself for your own parenting mishaps, you model healthy behavior for your children. Show them that it's okay not to be perfect and that self-kindness is a strength.

Encourage Exploration and Play: Provide opportunities for your children to explore their interests, play, and be creative without the pressure to perform or achieve specific outcomes. Exploration and play are crucial for cognitive, social, and emotional development.

Managing perfectionism in parenting is an ongoing process that requires mindfulness, reflection, and a willingness to grow. By balancing expectations and fostering a positive learning environment, Type 1 mothers can support their children's development into well-rounded, confident, and resilient individuals. This journey not only benefits the child but also offers Type 1 women an opportunity for personal growth, deepening their understanding of themselves and enriching their experience of motherhood. In embracing the imperfect journey of parenting, Type 1 mothers can find profound fulfillment and joy in watching their children grow and thrive in their own unique ways.

Conscious and Present Parenting: Strategies for Being Present and Consciously Involved in Parenting"

For Enneagram Type 1 women, navigating the realm of motherhood and parenting brings with it a unique set of aspirations and challenges. Known for their principled approach, strong sense of duty, and innate desire for improvement, Type 1 mothers often strive to embody the ideals of parenting perfection. However, the pursuit of perfection can sometimes overshadow the essence of parenting itself—being present and consciously involved in the lives of their children. Embracing conscious and present parenting offers Type 1 women a path to meaningful connection with their children, fostering a nurturing environment that supports mutual growth and understanding.

Understanding Conscious and Present Parenting

Conscious and present parenting is an approach that emphasizes awareness, mindfulness, and intentionality in the parenting journey. It encourages parents to engage deeply with their children, understanding their unique personalities, needs, and perspectives. For Type 1 women, this approach can be particularly transformative, as it shifts the focus from striving for an unattainable ideal to celebrating the beauty of the present moment and the authenticity of their children.

Strategies for Being Present and Consciously Involved

Embrace Imperfection: Recognize that perfection in parenting is an illusion. Embrace the imperfections of daily life and understand that making mistakes is a natural part of the parenting journey. This acceptance can liberate Type 1 mothers from the self-imposed pressure to be perfect, allowing them to be more present and engaged with their children.

Practice

Mindfulness: Incorporate mindfulness practices into your daily routine, both personally and as a family. Simple practices like mindful breathing, eating, and walking can help cultivate a state of presence that enriches interactions with your children. Mindfulness encourages a deeper connection, fostering an environment where children feel seen, heard, and valued.

Create Quality Time: Dedicate uninterrupted time to spend with your children, free from distractions such as work, technology, and household chores. Use this time to engage in activities that your children enjoy and that allow for meaningful conversations. Quality time strengthens the parent-child bond and demonstrates your commitment to being an active participant in their lives.

Listen Actively: Cultivate the art of active listening. When your children speak, give them your full attention, reflecting back their feelings and thoughts to show that you truly understand. Active listening validates their experiences and emotions, building trust and open communication.

Foster Autonomy and Exploration: Encourage your children to explore their interests, make decisions, and learn from their experiences. Supporting their autonomy respects their individuality and promotes self-confidence. For Type 1 mothers, this can also be a practice in releasing control and trusting in their children's ability to grow and learn in their unique ways.

Reflect and Adjust: Regularly reflect on your parenting approach and be willing to adjust based on the needs of your children and the dynamics of your family. Openness to change demonstrates a commitment to conscious parenting and ensures that your approach evolves as your children grow.

Conscious and present parenting is a journey of growth, not just for children but for parents as well. For Enneagram Type 1 women, embracing this approach offers an opportunity to soften the edges of perfectionism, creating space for more authentic, loving, and enriching experiences with their children. By being present and consciously involved, Type 1 mothers can nurture their children's development while also nurturing their own personal growth, ultimately realizing the profound joy and fulfillment that parenting can bring.

CHAPTER 6

Spirituality and Transcendence

"Spirituality and Transcendence: The Enneagram and Connection to the Universe"

For Type 1 women on the Enneagram, the journey toward spirituality and transcendence is deeply interwoven with their quest for integrity, order, and the embodiment of their highest ideals. The Enneagram, with its rich historical roots and profound psychological insights, serves as a unique tool for deepening one's spiritual connection, offering pathways to understanding the self and the universe in more meaningful ways. This chapter explores how the Enneagram can facilitate Type 1 women's spiritual growth and enhance their sense of connection to the cosmos.

The Enneagram as a Spiritual Mirror

At its core, the Enneagram reflects the universal truths and principles that underlie human nature and the cosmos. For Type 1 women, who are inherently driven by a desire for perfection and moral correctness, the Enneagram provides a mirror that reflects not only their strengths but also their limitations and the unconscious motivations that shape their worldview.

By engaging with the Enneagram as a spiritual tool, Type 1s can embark on a journey of self-discovery that transcends the ego, allowing them to connect more deeply with the essence of who they are beyond their personality type.

Embracing Imperfection as a Pathway to Growth

One of the most significant spiritual lessons for Type 1 women is the acceptance of imperfection. The Enneagram teaches that each type's greatest strength is also its greatest challenge. For Type 1s, the pursuit of perfection can become a barrier to spiritual growth if it prevents them from accepting the imperfection inherent in being human. By embracing their imperfections and viewing them as opportunities for growth and learning, Type 1 women can develop a more compassionate relationship with themselves and others, fostering a sense of grace and humility that is essential for spiritual transcendence.

Cultivating Mindfulness and Presence

The practice of mindfulness and presence is another aspect of the Enneagram's spiritual dimension that can profoundly benefit Type 1 women. Mindfulness practices encourage individuals to live in the present moment, observing their thoughts, emotions, and sensations without judgment. For Type 1s, who may be prone to self-criticism and a preoccupation with correcting flaws, mindfulness can provide a pathway to inner peace and a deeper connection to the spiritual essence of life. Through mindfulness, Type 1 women can learn to appreciate the beauty and perfection of the present moment, recognizing that the universe unfolds in its own perfect timing.

Connecting with the Universal through Service

Type 1 women are naturally inclined toward service and making a positive impact in the world. The Enneagram encourages this inclination by highlighting the interconnectedness of all life and the importance of serving the greater good. By engaging in acts of service, Type 1s can experience a profound sense of connection to the universal, realizing that their efforts contribute to the harmony and well-being of the cosmos.

This realization can elevate their sense of purpose and deepen their spiritual journey, affirming that their contributions are part of a larger, divine plan.

The Journey of Spiritual Transcendence

The Enneagram's capacity to facilitate spiritual growth and transcendence is a powerful resource for Type 1 women on their spiritual journey. By using the Enneagram as a guide for self-reflection and growth, Type 1s can navigate the complexities of their personalities, embrace their inherent imperfections, and cultivate a deeper connection to the spiritual essence of life. This journey of transcendence not only enriches their personal spiritual experience but also enhances their ability to contribute to the world in meaningful ways, embodying the highest expressions of their type.

In embracing the Enneagram as a tool for spiritual growth, Type 1 women can discover a path to transcendence that honors their unique strengths and challenges. Through this journey, they can realize their true, authentic selves and their integral connection to the universe, experiencing the profound beauty and harmony that lie at the heart of all existence.

Diverse Spiritual Practices: Incorporating a Variety of Spiritual Practices That May Resonate With Different Readers"

The spiritual journey is as unique as the individual embarking upon it, especially for Type 1 women, who seek alignment, purpose, and a deeper understanding of themselves and the universe. The Enneagram, with its deep roots in ancient wisdom and its application in modern personal growth, offers a foundation for exploring spirituality. This chapter introduces a variety of spiritual practices that may resonate with different readers, providing Type 1 women with a spectrum of tools to enhance their spiritual journey and transcendence.

1. Meditation and Mindfulness

Meditation and mindfulness practices offer profound paths to inner peace and self-awareness. For Type 1 women, who often grapple with an internal critic and high personal standards, these practices can be particularly liberating. Meditation provides a space to observe thoughts and emotions without judgment, fostering a deeper connection to the self and the present moment. Mindfulness, practiced throughout the day, can help in recognizing the beauty of the imperfect and the value of being rather than doing.

2. Nature Connection

Connecting with nature is a powerful spiritual practice that can help Type 1 women feel a sense of belonging to something greater than themselves. Activities such as walking in nature, gardening, or simply sitting and observing the natural world can provide moments of awe and wonder, grounding Type 1s in the present and offering a respite from the pursuit of perfection.

3. Journaling for Reflection

Journaling is a reflective practice that allows for the exploration of thoughts, feelings, and experiences. For Type 1 women, journaling can be a tool for self-discovery, offering a private space to confront the inner critic, reflect on personal growth, and document spiritual insights. Gratitude journaling, in particular, can shift focus from what needs to be improved to what is already whole and beautiful in life.

4. Sacred Reading

Engaging with spiritual texts, whether from religious traditions, philosophy, or personal growth literature, can provide Type 1 women with new perspectives and insights. Sacred reading invites contemplation and the exploration of universal truths, allowing Type 1s to connect with wisdom that transcends their personal experience and to reflect on the interconnectedness of all things.

5. Service and Acts of Kindness

For Type 1 women, who are naturally inclined towards improving the world, service can be a deeply fulfilling spiritual practice.

Volunteering, acts of kindness, and advocacy work offer pathways to transcend the self and contribute to the greater good. These actions can be expressions of spiritual beliefs in tangible form, affirming the interconnectedness of human experience and fostering a sense of purpose and belonging.

6. Creative Expression

Creativity is a spiritual practice that allows for the expression of the soul. For Type 1 women, creative activities such as painting, writing, music, or dance offer outlets for exploring and expressing their inner worlds. Engaging in creativity can be a form of meditation, a way to connect with the divine, and a method for navigating the journey of personal and spiritual growth.

7. Spiritual Community

Finding a community that shares spiritual values and practices can be incredibly supportive for Type 1 women. Whether through organized religion, spiritual study groups, or online communities, connecting with others on a spiritual path can provide encouragement, inspiration, and a sense of belonging. Community can also offer a mirror for personal growth, reflecting both the strengths and the areas of challenge that Type 1s face on their spiritual journey.

Incorporating diverse spiritual practices into their lives allows Type 1 women to explore different pathways to transcendence and to find practices that resonate with their unique spiritual needs. By engaging with these practices, Type 1s can deepen their connection to the universe, enhance their personal growth, and embrace the journey toward realizing their true, authentic selves. The Enneagram, as a guide to self-understanding and transformation, supports this journey, offering a holistic framework for spirituality and transcendence.

CHAPTER 7

YOUR WINGS

"The Wings of Enneagram Type One: Exploring the Influences of Type 1w9 and Type 1w2"

For Enneagram Type 1 women, known as The Perfectionists or Reformers, the nuances of their personalities are not solely defined by their core type. The adjacent types, or wings, play a significant role in shaping their complex character, preferences, and challenges. These wings—Type 9 (The Peacemaker) and Type 2 (The Helper)—add depth and diversity to the primary type, offering a broader spectrum of behaviors, motivations, and coping strategies. This section delves into how the wings influence Type 1 women, specifically focusing on Type 1w9 and Type 1w2.

Type 1w9: The Idealistic Peacemaker

Type 1w9s blend the principled and meticulous nature of Type 1 with the peace-seeking and accommodating qualities of Type 9. This combination results in individuals who are deeply driven by their ideals and values but approach their reformist tendencies with a calmer, more grounded demeanor compared to their Type 1 counterparts without a strong nine influence.

Personality and Preferences: Type 1w9 women are known for their serene and patient approach to life. They strive for improvement and perfection but are also able to see the bigger picture, often seeking harmony and balance in their surroundings. Their preference for peace over conflict makes them excellent mediators who can remain objective and composed, even in stressful situations.

Challenges: One of the main challenges for Type 1w9s is their tendency towards inertia. While they possess clear visions of how things should be, the Nine's influence can lead to procrastination or a reluctance to confront issues directly, especially if doing so might disrupt the peace. Balancing their desire for perfection with the need for practicality and acceptance can be a continuous struggle.

Strategies for Growth: For Type 1w9 women, growth comes from embracing action and assertiveness. Practicing decisiveness, even in small matters, can help overcome passivity. Additionally, cultivating mindfulness can aid in recognizing when the pursuit of peace is actually a form of avoidance, allowing them to address issues more directly.

Type 1w2: The Altruistic Reformer

Type 1w2s merge the high standards and ethical focus of Type 1 with the nurturing, people-oriented nature of Type 2. This combination creates individuals who not only strive for improvement and correctness but also place a strong emphasis on helping and connecting with others.

Personality and Preferences: Type 1w2 women are characterized by their warmth and genuine concern for others. They apply their reformist zeal not just to systems and processes but also to improving the lives of people around them. Their approach is often more interpersonal, with a preference for direct engagement in community or humanitarian efforts.

Challenges: The main challenge for Type 1w2s lies in balancing their own needs with their desire to help others. They may overextend themselves or neglect their well-being in the pursuit of being of service. Additionally, their inner critic can be particularly harsh, not only regarding their own actions but also in relation to whether they are doing enough for others.

Strategies for Growth: For Type 1w2 women, self-care is not selfish but essential. Learning to set boundaries and prioritize their well-being enables them to sustain their efforts to help others. Embracing self-compassion and recognizing the value of their contributions, regardless of their scale, can also mitigate the inner critic's impact.

The wings of Enneagram Type One offer a nuanced view of how Type 1 women navigate the world, highlighting the diversity within this personality type. Whether influenced by Type 9's peace-seeking nature or Type 2's altruistic tendencies, understanding and integrating these aspects can lead to a more balanced and fulfilled life. By acknowledging the strengths and challenges of their wings, Type 1 women can embark on a journey of personal growth that embraces the full spectrum of their complex personalities, leading them toward a more holistic realization of their true, authentic selves.

CHAPTER 8

WORKBOOK

Did you love *The woman of Enneagram 1: Love Marriage Success Edition*? Then you should read *The woman of enneagram 2*[1] by Maria Rondon!

[2]

Enneagram Type 2 Woman Discover the transformative power of the Enneagram as a Type 2 woman. This revealing book offers invaluable insights into the core motivations, strengths, and growth opportunities for the Giver personality type. As a Type 2 Enneagram woman, you strive to care for, understand, and support others in all aspects of life. While these qualities are commendable, they can also lead to neglecting your own needs, seeking external approval, and fearing being considered selfish. This book empowers you to embrace your true essence while freeing yourself from limiting patterns. Through provocative exercises and real-life examples, you'll explore how the Enneagram impacts your

---

1. https://books2read.com/u/b5J291

2. https://books2read.com/u/b5J291

relationships (Enneagram in Love, Enneagram in Marriage), your career, and your personal growth journey. Gain a deeper understanding of your drives, learn to care for yourself with the same intensity you care for others, and develop self-compassion and balance. If you're looking to improve your relationships, advance in your career, or simply live a more authentic and fulfilling life, this book is a powerful guide. It offers practical strategies and insights to help you leverage the strengths of your Type 2 personality while addressing your core fears and blind spots. Dive into this transformative book today and start a journey of self-discovery, personal empowerment (Enneagram Empowerment), and profound growth (Enneagram for Personal Growth). Unlock your true potential as an Enneagram Type 2 woman and live with greater presence, purpose, and inner peace.

Also by Maria Rondon

Alzheimer
Alzheimer Guia para cuidadores

Enneagram For Women
The woman of Enneagram 1: Love Marriage Success Edition
The woman of enneagram 2
The woman of Enneagram 3: Love marriage success edition
The Woman of Enneagram 4: Love, Marriage, Success Edition
The woman of Enneagram 5: Love marriage success edition
The Woman of Enneagram 6: Love, Marriage, Success Edition
The woman of Enneagram 7: Love marriage success edition
The woman of Enneagram 8: Love marriage success edition
The woman of Enneagram 9: Love marriage success edition

LOA
El secreto para atraer tu alma gemela